Water Dance

THOMAS LOCKER

Voyager Books • Harcourt, Inc.

ORLANDO AUSTIN NEW YORK SAN DIEGO TORONTO LONDON

SOME PEOPLE SAY that I am one thing.
Others say that I am many.
Ever since the world began
I have been moving in an endless circle.
Sometimes I fall from the sky.

I am the rain.

Sometimes I cascade.
I tumble
down,
down,
over the moss-covered rocks,
through the forest shadows.

I am the mountain stream.

At the foot of the mountains,
I leap from a stone cliff.
Spiraling.
Plunging.

I am the waterfall.

In the shadows of the mountain,
I am still and deep.
I fill
and overflow.

I am the lake.

I wind through broad, golden valleys
joined by streams,
joined by creeks.
I grow ever wider,
broader and deeper.

I am the river.

I pass through a gateway
of high stone palisades,
leaving the land behind.
Cool silver moonlight
sparkles and dances
on my waves.

I am the sea.

Drawn upward
by warm sunlight,
in white-silver veils
I rise into the air.
I disappear.

I am the mist.

In thousands of shapes I reappear
high above the earth in the blue sky.
I float.
I drift.

I am the clouds.

Carried by winds
from distant seas
I move,
growing heavier,
growing darker,
returning.

I am the storm front.

At the wall of the mountains,
I rise up
as gleaming power-filled towers
in the darkened sky.

I am the thunderhead.

I blind the sky with lightning.
The earth trembles with my thunder.
I rage.
I drench the mountainside.

I am the storm.

Storms come.
Storms pass.
I am countless droplets of rain
left floating in the silent air.
I reflect all the colors of sunlight.

I am the rainbow.

I am one thing.
I am many things.

I am water.

This is my dance through our world.

THE WATER CYCLE

WATER is so familiar that it is easy to take it for granted. Yet it is what makes the planet earth unique within the solar system. Water is the only substance on earth that naturally occurs in three different forms. At the Poles, it is huge masses of ice. In lakes, rivers, and oceans, it is liquid. In the atmosphere, reaching upward for many miles, it is vapor appearing as clouds, mist, and fog. Where rain is plentiful, there are rich tropical rainforests with lush soil, broad-leaved green plants, and colorful birds. When rain is scarce, deserts occur where cacti blossom in the sandy soil and lizards bask on sunbaked rocks. Each of these climates and the plants and animals that live in such regions are influenced by water. More than 70 percent of the earth's surface is covered by water, and your body is between 65 and 70 percent water.

Water moves through an endless journey between the earth and the sky. Clouds become falling rain that fills still mountain lakes, broad rivers, and underground streams. This journey of evaporation and condensation is called the water cycle. It purifies the water that sustains life on this blue planet. The amount of water on the earth has been almost the same for hundreds of millions of years. The water you used in your bath last night could have been in the Nile River last month. Only tiny amounts of new water are formed from the action of volcanoes and lightning.

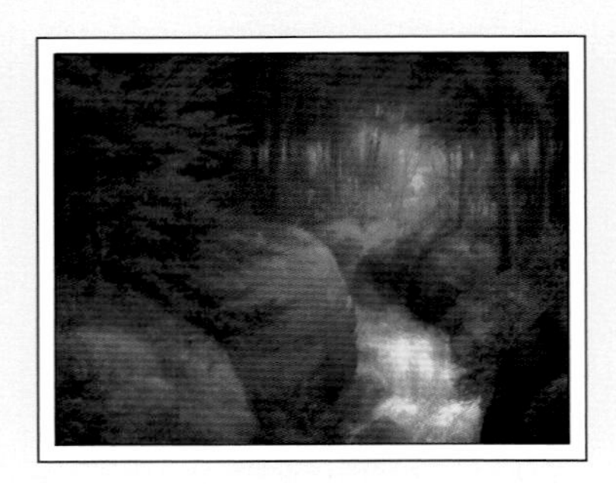

Water is pulled downward from mountain lakes and streams to the sea by the force of gravity. But water also moves in tides pulled by the force of the moon and is influenced by the warmth of the sun. Wind moving across the ocean's surface creates large rivers within the ocean called currents. When the sun warms the surface of a body of water, the water evaporates and moves upward as vapor.

The power of moving water is one of the forces that shapes the earth. Water's moving force, called erosion, slowly turns mountains into gracefully rounded hills. When it freezes, water can split huge boulders and carry stones and sand from the land to the sea. Even giant waterfalls are changed by water and slowly move backward upriver as water erodes the top rock away. Water is the sculptor of earth, creating canyons, gorges, waterfalls, broad river valleys, and rich fertile deltas on its journey to the sea.

If you look across a large lake or a broad river, you might wonder how much water there is in the whole world. Although there is a great deal of water in lakes and rivers, most of the planet's water is in the oceans, frozen as ice at the Poles, or lies deep beneath the earth in underground rivers. Only 3 percent of the world's water is actually the freshwater that living things need. Some precipitation soaks into the earth and becomes part of the groundwater supply. Groundwater moves beneath the earth's surface to bodies of water such as rivers and lakes. The water table is the top level of groundwater.

The great rivers that carry water throughout the lands begin as small streams of freshwater from rain, melting snow, or the emergence of underground springs. When many streams merge, they erode a deep bed that can hold more water and a river forms. Close to its source a river is usually narrow and deep, filled with rapids and waterfalls. As it travels, it begins to slow down and form graceful meanders through broad valleys .

Before it enters the sea, the river creates floodplains and rich deltas. Throughout this journey, it carries dissolved minerals and salts to the sea. The seas also have dissolved minerals from the earth beneath them. This salty seawater creates a favorable habitat for thousands of species. It is commonly thought that primitive life began in the waters of the ancient seas. The salty water provided food and warmth needed for life on earth to appear and flourish.

White clouds floating overhead, thick sticky fog on an autumn night, and gray clouds darkening the sky are different forms of water. Clouds and mists are formed when the sun warms the surface of the waters in lakes, streams, oceans, and puddles. Then water in the form of a gas rises into the warm air and a mist or fog appears. This is called evaporation.

The amount of water vapor in the air in combination with the wind and temperature determines the weather and climates on earth. The sun warms the planet unevenly, more at the equator and less at the Poles. Warm air flows from hotter to cooler areas. This flow and the movement of the earth create patterns of air movement called prevailing winds. As these large masses of air move, they affect each other at their borders or fronts. The difference between these great currents of air and gaseous water may cause soft spring rain, great thunderstorms, or even destructive tornadoes and hurricanes.

If water vapor continues to rise in the warmth of the sun, tiny droplets of water begin to collect around dust particles in the air. When these cool, a cloud is formed. Clouds are masses of water droplets and ice crystals in the atmosphere. They come in all shapes and sizes. *Cirrus clouds* look like thin feathers and tell us that the weather will be fair. Puffy *cumulus clouds* appear in fair weather, but when their centers turn gray, a storm might occur. Thick dark cloud blankets that form on gray days are called *stratus clouds.*

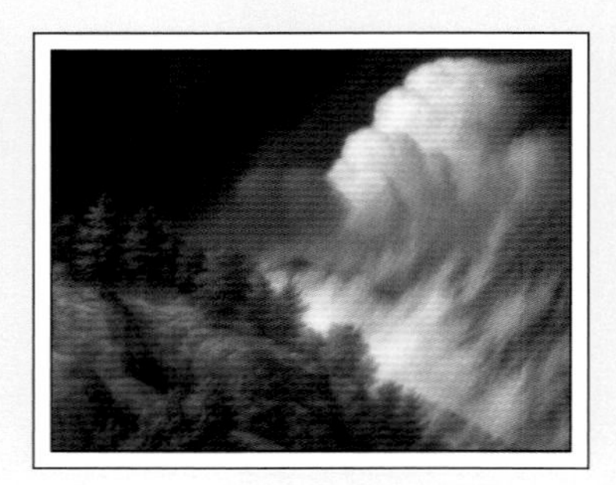

The power of the weather comes from the sun, the land, and the water. The sun's heat causes air to flow and swirl around the earth. Warm, moist air rises from the Tropics and cool, dry air flows down from the Poles. Ocean currents cool or warm the air; hills and mountains block the winds. Even the earth's rotation changes the direction of the moist or dry winds. Storms arise where air masses meet. When they meet, they do not mix. Instead, high winds and violent weather are created. When cold, dry air meets warm, moist air, it forces warmer air to rise quickly, producing updrafts and huge, dark thunderheads.

All the motion of ice crystals and water droplets inside of clouds creates tremendous energy. When clouds release this energy, millions of volts of static electricity are released in a blinding flash of lightning. The booming thunderclap that follows comes from the waves of air that expand after being heated by the electrical discharge.

Rainbows, sundogs, and moondogs are created by an interplay between water and sunlight or water and moonlight by processes called reflection and refraction. When light passes through water, or droplets of water, the results are the same as in a prism; the light does not travel straight but bends at an angle and is refracted. Also, light is separated into seven visible colors: red, orange, yellow, green, blue, indigo, and violet. When the sun is out during a light shower, or when there is moisture in the air, you can sometimes see these colors—in a rainbow.

At sunset the angle of the light passing through the atmosphere is different than when the sun is directly overhead at midday. Water vapor and dust particles reflect mostly blue light at noon. That is why the sky looks blue on a sunny day. At sunset light must travel a greater distance through the atmosphere as the sun sinks behind mountains, hills, or plains. When the evening light travels at an angle through many layers of water vapor and dust, the sky appears to be filled with beautiful orange and red lights.

Scientific information was researched and written by Candace Christiansen, who is the author of several books for children and has taught science for more than ten years.

www.HarcourtBooks.com

First Voyager Books edition 2002
Voyager Books is a trademark of Harcourt, Inc., registered in the United States of America and/or other jurisdictions.

The Library of Congress has cataloged the hardcover edition as follows:
Locker, Thomas, 1937–
Water dance/by Thomas Locker.
p. cm.
Summary: Water speaks of its existence in such forms as storm clouds, mist, rainbows, and rivers. Includes factual information on the water cycle.
[1. Water — Fiction. 2. Hydrologic cycle — Fiction.] I. Title.
PZ7.L7945Wat 1997
[Fic]—dc20 95-47861
ISBN 0-15-201284-2
ISBN 0-15-216396-4 pb

TWP Z Y X W V U T S R

The illustrations in this book were done in oils on canvas.
The text type was set in Goudy Italian Oldstyle.
The display type was set in Pablo.
Color separations by Bright Arts, Ltd., Singapore
Printed and bound by Tien Wah Press, Singapore
Production supervision by Sandra Grebenar and Wendi Taylor
Designed by Michael Farmer

Sparkling. Glistening. Roaring. Trickling.

Whooshing. Surging. Calming. Water.

Follow the planet's most precious resource—water—on its daily journey as it dances through our world.

"A happy marriage of art and science."—*School Library Journal*

"Locker's paintings and text are poetic."—*Kirkus Reviews*

"Lushly romantic oil paintings [and] poetic text, offer viewers a sensuous introduction to the water cycle."—*The Bulletin*

An IRA Teachers' Choice
An NCTE Notable Children's Trade Book in the Language Arts
An NSTA-CBC Outstanding Science Trade Book for Children

NEW!

Read all of Thomas Locker's books about nature.

Voyager Books
Harcourt, Inc.

www.HarcourtBooks.com

Printed in Singapore

Healthy Eating with MyPyramid

In 2005 the USDA unveiled MyPyramid to help Americans make healthier eating choices. MyPyramid, which replaces the old Food Guide Pyramid, stresses the need for individual food plans. The Healthy Eating with MyPyramid set explains each food group and gives healthy, tasty ideas for getting the nutrients you need every day.

www.capstonepress.com

What's on today's menu? Feed yourself a healthy serving of information about the fruit group.

Titles in Healthy Eating:

- Being Active
- Drinking Water
- The Fruit Group
- The Grain Group
- Healthy Snacks
- The Meat and Beans Group
- The Milk Group
- The Vegetable Group

Capstone Press – Pebble Plus

ISBN-13: 978-0-7368-6922-5
ISBN-10: 0-7368-6922-0
90000
9 780736 869225

Plus

Healthy Eating with MyPyramid

The Fruit Group

by Mari C. Schuh

Consulting Editor: Gail Saunders-Smith, PhD

Consultant: Barbara J. Rolls, PhD
Guthrie Chair in Nutrition
The Pennsylvania State University
University Park, Pennsylvania

Capstone press

Mankato, Minnesota

Pebble Plus is published by Capstone Press,
151 Good Counsel Drive, P.O. Box 669, Mankato, Minnesota 56002.
www.capstonepub.com

Printed in the United States of America in North Mankato, Minnesota.

005713R
022010

Library of Congress Cataloging-in-Publication Data
Schuh, Mari C., 1975–
The fruit group / by Mari C. Schuh.
p. cm.—(Pebble plus. Healthy eating with MyPyramid)
Summary: "Simple text and photographs present the fruit group, the foods in this group, and examples of healthy eating choices"—Provided by publisher.
Includes bibliographical references and index.
ISBN-13: 978-0-7368-5370-5 (hardcover)
ISBN-10: 0-7368-5370-7 (hardcover)
ISBN-13: 978-0-7368-6922-5 (softcover pbk.)
ISBN-10: 0-7368-6922-0 (softcover pbk.)
1. Fruit—Juvenile literature. 2. Nutrition—Juvenile literature. I. Title. II. Series.
TX558.F7S38 2006
641.3'4—dc22 2005023716

Credits
Jennifer Bergstrom, designer; Kelly Garvin, photo researcher; Stacy Foster and Michelle Biedscheid, photo shoot coordinators

Photo Credits
Capstone Press/Karon Dubke, cover, 1, 3, 5, 9, 11, 13, 15, 16–17, 19, 21, 22 (all)
Corbis/Claude Woodruff, 6–7; Michael Prince, 5 (background)
U.S. Department of Agriculture, 8, 9 (inset)

The author dedicates this book to her friend Liz Odom of Fairmont, Minnesota.

Information in this book supports the U.S. Department of Agriculture's MyPyramid for Kids food guidance system found at http://www.MyPyramid.gov/kids. Food amounts listed in this book are based on an 1,800-calorie food plan.

The U.S. Department of Agriculture (USDA) does not endorse any products, services, or organizations.

Note to Parents and Teachers

The Healthy Eating with MyPyramid set supports national science standards related to nutrition and physical health. This book describes and illustrates the fruit group. The images support early readers in understanding the text. The repetition of words and phrases helps early readers learn new words. This book also introduces early readers to subject-specific vocabulary words, which are defined in the Glossary section. Early readers may need assistance to read some words and to use the Table of Contents, Glossary, Read More, Internet Sites, and Index sections of the book.

Table of Contents

Fruit

Fruit helps keep you
healthy and strong.
What fruit have
you eaten today?

Do you ever wonder
where fruit comes from?
Fruit grows on trees,
bushes, and vines.

MyPyramid for Kids

MyPyramid teaches you
how much to eat
from each food group.
Fruit is a food group
in MyPyramid.

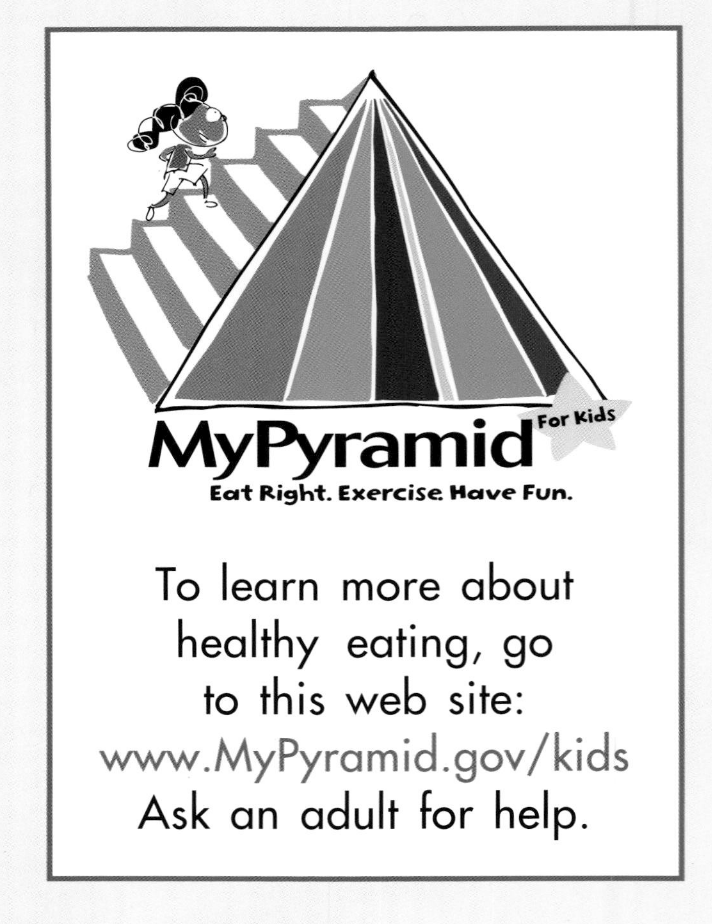

To learn more about
healthy eating, go
to this web site:
www.MyPyramid.gov/kids
Ask an adult for help.

http://teamnutrition.usda.gov/Resources/mpk_poster.pdf
MyPyramid
Grains
Vegetables
Fruits
Milk
Meat & Beans
SUN-MAID
NATURAL CALIFORNIA
RAISINS

Kids should eat
about 1½ cups of fruit
every day.

Enjoying Fruit

Yellow, orange, red.
How many colors
can you eat?
Enjoy bananas, oranges,
and apples.

Pears, melons, grapefruit.
Fruit comes in
many shapes and sizes.
Try a fruit you've never
eaten before.

1199
599

Strawberries make
a good snack
to share with a friend.

Sip, slurp, gulp.
Enjoy a cold fruit smoothie.
Smoothies have lots of fruit
in them.

Fruit makes a sweet part
of a healthy lunch.
What are your favorite fruits?

How Much to Eat

Kids need to eat about 1½ cups of fruit every day. To get 1½ cups, pick three of your favorite fruits below.

Pick three of your favorite fruits to enjoy today!

½ cup + ½ cup + ½ cup = 1½ cups

Glossary

fruit—the fleshy, juicy part of a plant; fruit has seeds.

MyPyramid—a food plan that helps kids make healthy food choices and reminds kids to be active; MyPyramid was created by the U.S. Department of Agriculture.

smoothie—a thick, smooth drink made by mixing milk, low-fat yogurt, and fruit in a blender

snack—a small amount of food people eat when they are hungry between meals

Read More

Klingel, Cynthia Fitterer, and Robert B. Noyed. *Fruit.* Let´s Read About Food. Milwaukee: Weekly Reader Early Learning Library, 2002.

Nelson, Robin. *Fruits.* First Step Nonfiction. Minneapolis: Lerner, 2003.

Rondeau, Amanda. *Fruits Are Fun.* What Should I Eat? Edina, Minn.: Abdo, 2003.

Index

Word Count: 126
Grade: 1
Early-Intervention Level: 14

Internet Sites

FactHound offers a safe, fun way to find Internet sites related to this book. All of the sites on FactHound have been researched by our staff.

Here's how:

1. Visit *www.facthound.com*
2. Type in this special code **0736853707** for age-appropriate sites. Or enter a search word related to this book for a more general search.
3. Click on the **Fetch It** button.

FactHound will fetch the best sites for you!